Original title:
The Attic of Forgotten Dreams

Copyright © 2025 Creative Arts Management OÜ
All rights reserved.

Author: Jasper Montgomery
ISBN HARDBACK: 978-1-80587-055-5
ISBN PAPERBACK: 978-1-80587-525-3

Whispers of Dusty Shadows

In corners where the shadows creep,
A stuffed bear snorts, and begins to peep.
Old hats dance in a breeze so light,
Challenging dust bunnies to a pillow fight.

An umbrella's laughing, just for fun,
As if it's waiting for a rain-soaked run.
Books stacked high, with stories to tell,
Whisper, 'Maybe we should cast a spell!'

Echoes of Childlike Laughter

A marble rolls and gives a chime,
Recalling games that felt like prime.
Jump ropes swing with giggling zeal,
As if they dream of youth's appeal.

Peeking out from beneath the floor,
An action figure begs for one more score.
Socks launch from shelves, a playful fight,
Squealing through memories, oh what a sight!

Nostalgia's Frayed Edges

Pictures fade but smiles remain,
An album's waiting to entertain.
Old video games chuckle and sneer,
"Remember when we had no fear?"

A bike with a flat still whines in glee,
Promising rides that used to be free.
A cap from a soda gives off a puff,
"Let's pop the cork, it's never enough!"

Secrets Wrapped in Cobwebs

Beneath the webs, secrets do twirl,
A crooked doll starts to twirl.
A shoebox holds treasures, locked tight,
Empty candy wrappers take flight!

Glasses of milk left out to dry,
Toasting to dreams that never say bye.
A clock ticks backward, time takes a break,
While jellybeans giggle, oh what a cake!

Chests of Hidden Longing

In the corner, a chest lays bare,
Filled with old shoes that never were a pair.
Tangled in sweaters that are two sizes small,
Do they fit my dreams, or are they just a wall?

A racing bike from a year long past,
Its tires are flat, and its youth didn't last.
Funny how memories can rust with grace,
Like a polka-dotted hat that once ruled this space.

A Yarn of Fading Joys

A spool of thread unwinds in glee,
Caught in a web of absurdity.
Knitted together, a sock with a hole,
Who knew such mischief could steal the whole roll?

A curtain of dreams, faded like cheese,
Whispering secrets that tickle and tease.
A dance of dust bunnies in bright summer light,
Polar bears in pajamas enjoy the sight.

Crumbling Hopes in Dim Light

On a shelf, the trophies gather dust,
But who was the champion? It's all a bust!
Winners once raged on the field so bold,
Now they just gather tales to be told.

An old lamp flickers with a cheeky grin,
Its light knows secrets and where it has been.
A picture of laughter caught in a frame,
Where everyone's smiling, but none are the same.

Fragments of Shattered Glass

Shards of laughter scatter on the floor,
Each piece a memory that echoes and roars.
A mirror reflects the confusion of time,
Who's the funny one? I'm lost in this rhyme.

A rusty old bike with a wheel askew,
Wondering if its bubble days are still true.
We chase after dreams, like kittens in yarn,
But who's to say we can't have some charm?

The Stillness of Silent Desires

In shadows lurk those wishes bold,
Yet here they sit, all dust and cold.
A bicycle waits, its tires flat,
Longing for rides, oh where's the cat?

A jester's hat, with bells that ring,
Dreams of laughter wrapped in spring.
A rubber chicken, bright and cheery,
Competes with hopes that make us weary.

The ice cream cone? Melted away,
Tales of flavors gone astray.
Hiccups of giggles, trapped in air,
Echoes of fun in disrepair.

Yet in the gloom, a chuckle flies,
For every sigh a laugh implies.
In dust we find, not grief, but glee,
Each forgotten wish, a jolly spree.

Whispers Beneath the Beams

Beneath the beams where secrets dwell,
A sock puppet sings, oh what a swell!
It tells of tales of knights in foam,
And dragons made of tinfoil chrome.

A ukulele with three strings left,
Plays songs of silly, half-hearted theft.
A clam that dreams of being a star,
In the oceans of jelly like a quirky czar.

There's a sandwich, half-eaten, it seems,
With mustard thoughts and pickle dreams.
The clock ticks loud, yet laughs it plays,
As whispers dance in the sun's warm rays.

With every tick, those giggles swell,
In corners where wild fantasies dwell.
Oh, what a life with dreams so bright,
Even quiet corners spark delight!

An Echo in the Dark

In the dark there's a squeaky wheel,
A rubber band comes to steal the feel.
Echoes of laughter in echoes confined,
As whispers of longing unwind and unwind.

A ghost made of laundry, hung just so,
With ambitions to be a fashion show.
It twirls and spins, yet makes no sound,
A comedian lost, in the threads it's found.

Old toys once loved now mumble and sigh,
A rattle croons, 'Oh, me? Oh my!'
With every thump in the dusty night,
The shadows break into sheer delight.

Through the giggles of old forgotten beams,
An echo shines through the tangled dreams.
In quiet corners, the fun won't cease,
For even in silence, there's a vibrant peace!

Tattered Pages of Lost Time

Tattered pages, a book once bright,
Filled with doodles that lift the night.
Bigfoot danced on a roller skate,
While unicorns stole a slice of fate.

A scribble here, a coffee stain there,
The plot goes missing, nobody cares.
A treasure map to the couch's end,
Where the lost socks and giggles blend.

Stories of tacos that fly through space,
And pirate ducks in a grand parade race.
Each line a riddle, a silly escape,
From serious life, it crafts a new shape.

As laughter peeks through the creased pages,
Whimsical thoughts of all ages.
In the margins, dreams never fade,
For every miss is a jolly crusade!

Echoes of a Whispered Hope

In shadows where lost wishes sleep,
A goldfish plans its leap.
It dreams of swimming in the sky,
But flops instead and wonders why.

Crumpled papers float about,
Like secret snacks—no doubt!
A toast to dreams that slip and slide,
Bouncing back with silly pride.

In corners where old tales reside,
A rubber chicken takes a ride.
With wobbly legs, it dances free,
To silly tunes of jubilee.

Yet as the laughter starts to soar,
A dust bunny locks the door.
With whispered jokes and giggly schemes,
It guards the vault of silly dreams.

Serendipity in Dust Bunnies

Amidst the fluff of timeless dust,
Lie dreams once stored, now lost in rust.
A sock puppet waves and grins,
While an old shoe jars with whims.

A treasure map drawn in coffee stains,
Leads to a stash of candy canes.
With giggles tucked in every crease,
Adventures start, the laughs increase.

Silver spoons fight with rusty forks,
Debating who's the king of dorks.
As giggling whispers fill the air,
The dust bunnies join the silly flair.

In the quiet where dreams may twirl,
Old teddy bears begin to swirl.
With mismatched charm, they sway along,
To the rhythm of a playful song.

Silhouettes of Silent Aspirations

In shadows cast by ancient beams,
Silly ghosts perform their dreams.
Yet socks and hats have lost their flair,
While rubber bands hang in mid-air.

A scarf wraps haste 'round a dusty chair,
Claiming it's too shy to share.
With silent hopes that twinkle bright,
They plot an escape into the night.

Juggling dreams, a cat takes flight,
On tiny paws—what a sight!
With every leap, a cheer resounds,
As laughter echoes through the grounds.

But when morning arrives, they hide,
In nooks where silly dreams reside.
Where shadows stretch and giggle low,
The wishes dance, and laughter flows.

Riddles Beneath the Rafters

Above the world, where time is still,
Riddles hang in the dusty chill.
A hat asks questions, a shoe replies,
While a mirror giggles with surprise.

A kazoo plays nonsensical tunes,
As spoons compete with mischievous moons.
Each corner holds a puzzle tight,
With whispers dancing in the light.

In a forgotten box of cheer,
A rubber ducky waves from here.
With beaks that quack in playful jest,
It's time for dreams to frolic best.

So raise a toast to all that's odd,
To hidden tales of every sod.
For in the laughter, hope persists,
Beneath the beams, where joy insists.

The Chests of Yesteryear's Wishes

In a chest of old, I found a shoe,
It seems I wished for a dance or two.
Next to it, a hat with feathers so bright,
I dreamed of fame, and glittery light.

A pocket watch is ticking, but it's stuck,
I wished for time to change my luck.
Among candy wrappers and broken toys,
I giggle at the innocence of my joys.

A diary filled with doodles and names,
What were those wild, silly games?
Unopened letters from a crush long lost,
The dreams were sweet; oh, what a cost!

With silly dreams sprawled across the floor,
I laugh at wishes I can't ignore.
Perhaps tomorrow, I'll dust them off,
And plan a hilarious do-over scoff.

Murmurs from the Overhead

I heard a whisper from up on high,
Was it a ghost, or the dust bunnies' sigh?
They chatter about the socks they've spied,
One lonely pair that's long since dried.

Above my head, a spider spins webs,
Filling the air with quirky celeb
Stories of knots and untangled dreams,
I chuckle at plans that burst at the seams.

Bottles of wishes hang from the beams,
Rusty and faded, they still hold dreams.
One's labeled 'Cereal for Dinner,' oh wow,
My dreams were wild, but what happened now?

The rafters giggle with secrets untold,
Each echo a memory, dusty but bold.
With shadows and laughter, a raucous crew,
These murmurs remind me of who I once knew.

Shadows of Unspoken Longing

In corners where cobwebs find a home,
Shadows dance and giggle 'neath the dome.
The dreams of a space ranger lost in time,
Floating about in a galactic rhyme.

An old teddy bear with a quirky grin,
Once a brave knight, now hiding within.
He whispers tales of daring flight,
But sticks to the shadows, away from the light.

A love letter tucked in a dusty nook,
Words so cheesy, they'd make someone crook.
The longing unvoiced, but oh-so-clear,
A quaint little crush; hold the laughter near!

These shadows of mine waltz through the day,
As I unlock their jokes in a cheerful way.
Life is a comedy wrapped in a mystery,
Dreams that linger entertain my history.

Cluttered Visions of a Bygone Age

A jumble of hats and a pair of old skates,
Visions of grandeur that my heart still awaits.
Piled in a corner, like thoughts in my head,
Each piece a chuckle for the dreams that I've fed.

There's a yo-yo that spins with a flourish,
Once a magician, now covered in nourish.
Giggling at clown shoes tucked underneath,
The silliness sprouts with each hidden wreath.

I flip through the pages of comic book lore,
Laughter erupts from the tales of yore.
Superheroes saving with joy and delight,
Adventures still calling me into the night.

These cluttered visions, a riotous spree,
Tickle my heart like a sprightly bee.
With laughter and memories quietly stacked,
I embrace the foolishness—life is quite whacked!

The Muffled Symphony of Hesitations

In a corner, socks dance and twirl,
While the clock just snoozes in a curl.
Thoughts get tangled, like old string,
Humming softly, lost in the spring.

Pants that never fit me just right,
Whisper their secrets in the night.
A tune of doubts, a laugh, a sigh,
As the dust bunnies make their reply.

The old guitar plays a rusty tune,
While lost bananas become a monsoon.
Faded dreams shake hands with the past,
Waving goodbye, they move way too fast.

In this place where silence plays,
Every hesitation has its ways.
The laughter's muffled, yet it's near,
As I trip over the thoughts I fear.

A Dandelion's Last Wish

Once a flower so bold and bright,
Danced with the breeze; what a sight!
Now it dreams of being a star,
But finds itself stuck in a jar.

Puffed up wishes float through the air,
While socks with holes sit in despair.
'Oh to be free!' the dandelion cries,
As a cat ponders life—paws in disguise.

It whispers secrets to passing bees,
'If I could fly, I'd visit the seas!'
But alas, it's stuck in this dusty nook,
Might need a plan—like a storybook.

With a pop, the dandelion departs,
Spreading laughter, joy to all hearts.
And I sit here, giggling along,
At the thought of a wish that went wrong.

Unreachable Stars Above the Dust

The stars twinkle like mischievous sprites,
But they trip over clouds in their flights.
I reach for one, but it giggles away,
Laughing at me, 'Try another day!'

Mismatched socks and an old rubber band,
Dreams of burgers up in the strand.
I ponder my fate in the cosmos above,
Stuck with these thoughts—not near any love.

The moon winks at the mess I've amassed,
As I chase dreams that never hold fast.
Dust bunnies whisper the secrets they keep,
While I wonder why stars don't jump or leap.

In this corner, glittering and bright,
Feels like a circus, all day and night.
So here's to the stars—so far, yet so close,
I'll dance with their shadows, I suppose!

The Silent Harbor of Lost Ideas

In a dusty corner, thoughts drift and sway,
Like tumbleweeds lost on a lazy day.
Cotton candy clouds sit on the floor,
While a toast to the dreams that were never more.

An idea so grand, it trips on a shoe,
While others just giggle, 'Oh, how untrue!'
A laugh escapes from a forgotten hat,
As I wonder where on earth it sat.

Paper boats sail on puddles of thought,
They paddle away to the battles I've fought.
But here in the harbor, tucked under a beam,
The mirth of lost plans clinks like a dream.

So, raise a cup to ideas gone wild,
As I sit on the floor, like a silly child.
In this silent harbor, where giggles abound,
Every tripped-up thought is honored and found.

Unraveled Threads of Hope

In a box of mismatched socks,
Lies a treasure of lost thoughts.
Frayed edges and tangled knots,
Dreams dance like firefly spots.

A rubber duck with three left shoes,
Tells tales of forgotten blues.
Puzzles without pieces muse,
Guessing games we cannot lose.

A noodle that might have been spaghetti,
Sets the stage for a grand confetti.
With hats made of crumpled confetti,
We laugh till our hearts feel heavy.

So take a peek in dusty nooks,
Where laughter hides and memory cooks.
For every whimsy in our books,
Are threads of joy in snazzy looks.

Cracked Frames of Once-Warm Wishes

A frame that holds a lopsided grin,
Remembers smiles long lost within.
Each crack a tale of where it's been,
While old hopes flutter like a tin.

Once a wish upon a star,
Now it waits in a rusty jar.
It laughs at dreams that wandered far,
But still believes they're who they are.

Paintings of cats that sing all day,
With whiskers bright, they dance and sway.
In yesteryear's light, they lose their way,
Yet still charm hearts in their play.

So here's to whims that left a trace,
In cracked frames of a warm embrace.
Our laughter echoes in this space,
As forgotten wishes find their place.

Hibernating Hopes Among the Beams

In the corner, a chair sits wide,
With blankets draped like dreams inside.
It giggles softly, not one to hide,
In the dust, all laughter's bide.

Among the rafters, a teddy bear's sown,
Telling secrets to the polka dot phone.
With chuckles and sighs, they've grown,
In a world of hopes that were once shown.

The ceiling sings of journeys past,
Where every wish was free to cast.
They've hibernated, but love holds fast,
Awaiting spring when fun's amassed.

So join the party of forgotten glee,
Where dreams take naps and sip on tea.
In the beams where shadows flee,
Lies laughter waiting to be free.

Echoes of a Dreamer's Heart

An old guitar strummed in the dark,
Hums of laughter, a cheeky spark.
It whispers tales from the park,
Where dreams once flew like a lark.

Pages flutter of a story untold,
Unraveling tales of spaghetti sold.
In margins, doodles brave and bold,
Reflecting mishaps we once controlled.

A chorus of socks, mismatched and bright,
Sing of whimsies through the night.
With every note, the world feels light,
Underneath the twinkling starlight.

So let the echoes take their part,
In the dance of a dreamer's heart.
With laughter woven in every chart,
We surely all can play our part.

Time's Neglected Corners

In a box of dad's old ties,
A cat's tangled in a flight.
Socks that danced with mismatched glee,
Whisper secrets of the night.

There's a chair that's missing a leg,
It claims it had too much fun.
Piles of dreams that never took flight,
Dancing 'til the morning sun.

A cap that thinks it's a crown,
Dust bunnies playfully unite.
Each cobweb tells a funny tale,
Of things that vanished from sight.

In corners where the laughter laid,
A treasure trove of all things weird.
With every laugh, a memory's made,
In the chaos, joy is cleared.

Fragments of a Faded Past

A photo of a chicken dance,
From years when style was quite bizarre.
Grandpa's bike that lost its chance,
Now holds the dust, not a car.

A diary filled with doodles bright,
Of crushes and snacks from 1990.
It whispers, 'I just might,
Write you songs that are quite shifty.'

A shoe that never got the pair,
Hiding secrets of a squirrel's plot.
And crayons made of long-lost flair,
Sketch visions of what we forgot.

In this maze of jumbled glee,
Oddities dance in goofy form.
Each chuckle sparks a memory,
In the chaos, laughter's warm.

Lost Lanterns of Memory

A lantern that fizzles with giggles,
Hides tales of jests long since passed.
It sways as the old song wriggles,
In a waltz from the distant cast.

A rubber chicken squawks out loud,
From the shelf where the dusty snacks lay.
It dreams of impressing a crowd,
But only the mice come to play.

A postcard pulled from yesteryears,
Showcases terrible beach hair.
Unicorns and macaroni spheres,
Find laughter in a world unfair.

These lanterns light up the attic,
Where silliness reigns supreme.
With every flicker dramatic,
We revive the joy of a dream.

Reveries Beneath the Eaves

Beneath the eaves where dreams conspire,
A sock puppet tells its tale.
With crooked stitches, it claims desire,
To join the dust and never fail.

A broken clock that lost its time,
Ticks in rhythm with a giggle.
While spiders weave a silly rhyme,
Around the eggs of a wiggly wiggle.

Forgotten toys with lots to say,
Conspire in a soft array.
They're plotting there to dance all day,
In this forgotten, funny fray.

In laughter's glow, the memories we find,
Slide through shadows, bright and keen.
In corners where we left behind,
The dreams that spark a goofy scene.

The Dusty Vault of What-Could-Have-Been

There's a hat made of stale cheese,
Just waiting for a brave soul's tease.
It promises fame and golden glory,
But sits instead, gathering dust and worry.

A pair of shoes, one left, one right,
Dance only in dreams, and hide from sight.
They claim they'll waltz on moonlit floors,
Instead, they just trip over old scores.

An accordion plays a tune so sour,
Reminding of parties that missed their hour.
The songs it sings are off-key and rough,
Yet it insists, 'let's party! Enough is enough!'

In this vault of delight, so full of fun,
Lies a treasure that nobody's begun.
Each item whispers a tale, makes you grin,
Of adventures lost where no one's been.

Windows Closed to Tomorrow

Peeking through the curtains tightly drawn,
Dreams of flying, but never at dawn.
The cat on the windowsill sighs in defeat,
It no longer believes in things that are sweet.

Pigeons coo with tips on how to soar,
While the clock rolls back like it's done before.
Can time really be trapped in baked beans?
It's all a confusion of odd little scenes.

A squirrel in a jacket checks his watch,
He's late for a party, or maybe a botch.
His tiny little plans slip and slide,
As he bobbles around on this hapless ride.

With windows shut tight, dreams fade away,
Hiding beneath pillows where they used to play.
But if you listen closely, you might hear a cue,
A chuckle from dreams saying, 'We still love you!'

Quests Lost in Time

A knight with a fridge as his trusty steed,
Gallops through valleys in search of a need.
He seeks the grail but finds just a snack,
A leftover pizza, the true treasure's lack.

Mermaids in bathtubs are brewing a stew,
While pirates argue over who's got the clue.
Their map isn't inked, just drawn in crayon,
Leading to fountains of warm chili con carne.

Dinosaurs play cards on the lawn,
Cheating at poker from dusk until dawn.
But the bets are just pebbles and tiny lost toys,
In a game of imagination filled with strange joys.

Time travelers meet in a coffee shop line,
Seeking adventures but stuck here for wine.
They laugh at the past, raise a toast to the fun,
And wonder out loud if their quest's ever done.

Abandoned Pages of Past Lives

Old stories wander like cats in the night,
Chasing their tails in the dim candlelight.
Each page a giggle, each line a sigh,
Funny how they choke when they try to fly.

In corners, they whisper their bright little tales,
Of pirates who sailed on ships made of snails.
Their treasure chests burst with mints and gumdrops,
Not gold but laughter, forever it plops.

A romance novel tangled in fairy floss threads,
Filled with hedgehogs who wear fancy reds.
They flirt with a pepper shaker, it's odd,
Yet tales of their love leave everyone nod.

These pages forgotten still dance on the shelf,
Holding their secrets like dear little elves.
A giggle escapes from a dusty old tome,
Each story a spark of home sweet home.

Memories Encased in Cobwebs

Up high, dusty dreams do dwell,
Where giggles hide and whispers swell.
A toy soldier stands, his paint all cracked,
Next to a sock—whose match is nacked.

A bike with flat tires, it surely seems,
Is longing for far-off, wild schemes.
A crooked hat from a jester's prank,
Hides a grin that's more rank than dank.

Where comic books gather dust and tears,
And old records hold all our fears.
A calendar stuck on Valentine's Day,
Where love went up the chimney, hey!

A treasure chest locked tight with glue,
Filled with crayons that once were blue.
In this place where time takes a nap,
Laughter echoes—take a break, take a lap!

Remnants of Once-Bright Visions

In the corner, dreams have crumbled there,
Packed in boxes without a care.
Plans for greatness with wild ideas,
Now serve as props for the dust bunnies' cheers.

A platform shoe that never found a chance,
Stagnant like hopes that refuse to dance.
The curtain's drawn on the grand parade,
Where tall stories faded, now displayed.

An old trophy that once shone so bright,
Is a paperweight in the dead of night.
While rubber bands twist like fate unkind,
Remnants of dreams with a giggling mind.

Laughter once echoed in every nook,
Now just shadows where jokers once took.
Yet in each crevice, a chuckle remains,
Of fading moments still wrapped in chains.

The Space Between Hopes and Reality

Up in the gloom, dreams play hide and seek,
With bravado they flaunt, yet stay so meek.
Crafts of paper and glue, once our pride,
Now awkward reminders sit sidelong outside.

Invisible bridges connect every tale,
But spiders weave webs that weave a new veil.
A sandwich lies waiting in a lunchbox so dear,
But picked up by squirrels once no one was near.

An umbrella with holes dreams of sunny days,
While mismatched socks celebrate in their ways.
Lost crayons take refuge, the colors are rare,
Each hue a reflection of what's lingering there.

This space is a circus, clowns laughing loud,
While hopes juggle dreams, feeling quite proud.
So tiptoe in quietly, bring laughter to light,
In the place where the bizarre and humor unite!

Faded Footsteps on Forgotten Paths

Footsteps echo with a comedy tune,
Leading to places where hopes ended soon.
Mint-condition gadgets, now looks quite sad,
Once the envy of all, now just an old fad.

A map with no sense, all routes curvy,
Leads a lost traveler feeling quite nervy.
Each corner explored with chuckles anew,
'Cross a field of dreams where the shadows grew.

Piles of journals with entries undone,
Stories of laughter, adventures, and fun.
Yet scribbles on pages in blue, red, and green,
Show the quirks of our lives, how wild they have been.

So throw wide the door, let the giggles commence,
On this path of the old, where dreams oft dispense.
Wipe off the dust, hear the laughter's swirl,
In the dance of yesterdays, let joy unfurl!

The Lantern's Glow on Shattered Dreams

A lantern flickers, shadows dance,
Old hats and mittens leap by chance.
The dreams we tossed on a lopsided shelf,
Whisper their secrets, giggling themselves.

A rubber chicken with a silly grin,
Says, "Get up, buddy! It's time to begin!"
In the dust of forgotten, we find a clue,
That laughter's a treasure, let's claim it anew.

Cobwebs wear wigs, oh what a sight!
They gossip and bicker through the night.
Forgotten ambitions with popcorn and zest,
Watch out world, we're ready for the next quest!

So here's to the whimsy, the fun we forgot,
In the attic of nonsense, a terrific spot!
With each silly dream that hangs like a ghost,
We toast to the laughter—yes, that's what we'll boast!

Vast Skies of Unclaimed Possibility

A paper plane drifts from the past,
Wishing on dreams that never did last.
It loops and spins with a giggle so bright,
Saying, "Why not soar? It's a beautiful flight!"

The dust bunnies dance, in a conga line,
With mismatched socks sipping lemonade fine.
While worlds of the mundane float by like a tease,
They shout, "Take a chance, do as you please!"

Forgotten ambitions float on balloons,
Singing silly songs of forgotten tunes.
With each breeze a giggle, a wink in the air,
"Why not unleash all your wildest flair?"

So let's break the glass of seriousness tight,
Dive into laughter, take off in delight.
With skies ever open and dreams in a swirl,
We'll dance with the silly—let's give them a twirl!

Echoes of Joy Encased in Stillness

In corners of peace, laughter winks wide,
A teddy bear chuckles; what a wild ride!
With echoes of joy wrapped in bright fluff,
They gather like stories; isn't that enough?

A mismatched clock ticks in reverse style,
It giggles and guffaws, keeps time with a smile.
While dreams we tucked away, start to play fair,
Pretending to chase shadows, without a care!

So here's to the echoes that bounce in your mind,
To wishful thoughts drifting, unconfined.
With a jiggle and chuckle, the stillness will break,
As dreams dance around, it's all for the take!

Let's gather the smiles that lurk in the gloom,
And pop them like bubbles—they'll fill up the room!
In the quietest moments, find joy's sweetest thrill,
For laughter encased is the best kind of fill!

The Forgotten Nook of Reflection

In a corner, dust bunnies play,
Chasing memories all day.
Mismatched shoes, a hat bizarre,
Who knew they'd travel so far?

A broken clock ticks with glee,
Counting moments, just for me.
Old photos line the wall with pride,
Oh, the secrets they can't hide!

A giggled ghost gives a wink,
Sipping shadows while I think.
Last week's cake sits in a chair,
Slightly stale, yet always there!

Among the junk, a rubber duck,
Whimsical luck or just sheer luck?
A treasure trove of silly sighs,
Oh, what joy when laughter flies!

Reflections in a Silent Chamber

In the stillness, whispers dance,
Caught in an odd circumstance.
A sock puppet gives a shout,
"Why'd you leave me out, no doubt!"

Dusty books with tales untold,
Clothes from fashion days of old.
They murmur softly in the night,
Sharing giggles, pure delight.

A mirror cracks but won't give in,
Reflecting tales of where we've been.
"Is that my hair?" I laugh and stare,
Replaying moments, unaware!

Chairs sit empty, oh so grand,
Adventurers lost, too far to stand.
Yet echoes of fun fill the air,
In each crevice, humor's flair!

Hues of Distant Dreams

Paint splatters tell a wild tale,
Of wishes missed like ships that sail.
A crumpled map with paths untread,
Leads to laughter instead of dread.

Painted skies, a silly hue,
With smiling clouds that wave on cue.
A teacup bird sings out a tune,
While the moon dons a laughing rune!

Dancing brushes, colors collide,
Creating joy we can't divide.
Stuck to walls, notes of jest,
Dreams gone funny, life's the best!

In every corner, cheer's abound,
While hope's giggle bounces around.
Let's toast to dreams, both bright and weird,
Where every wish is simply cheered!

The Remains of Untravelled Paths

A suitcase sits, no places known,
Full of socks and dreams overgrown.
With every zip, a memory plays,
Of wacky trips in silly ways!

Maps unfold, but not a clue,
To a world where no one flew.
Sad rubber bands wish for a trip,
Yet from the shelf, they can't quite slip!

In the shadows, a carpe diem,
But can't leave home, oh what a whim!
A dusty globe spins with a sneeze,
At lost adventures, all in tease.

Old road signs point nowhere bright,
But laughter's found in every bite.
Here's to paths we didn't take,
In our hearts, we still can shake!

Journeys Never Begun

An old suitcase sits with a frown,
Hoping to escape this dusty town.
Tags from journeys yet to take,
Instead, it just holds leftover cake.

A map rolled tight now bends,
Guiding nowhere, where laughter ends.
With every fold, a joke unspools,
As adventure waits in silly schools.

Forgotten tickets, a train departs,
But empty seats have playful hearts.
Dreams wrapped tight in comic fate,
Scribbled notes that just can't wait.

Plans elope with mismatched socks,
Adventure lives in paradox blocks.
These whimsical quests simply tease,
In the realm of dreams, where giggles seize.

Tangles of Unwritten Stories

A quill lays down a dance of dust,
Dreams untouched, but has to trust.
Ink spills laughter on the page,
With tales of spaghetti and a tiny sage.

Wonders wait in tangled threads,
Telling secrets, but no one spreads.
A chapter lost in silly schemes,
Finding joy in half-baked dreams.

Characters run, but then they trip,
On banana peels, they lose their grip.
Each plot twist, a tickling race,
In a land where nonsense finds its place.

Papers flutter like butterflies,
Whispering outlandish alibis.
Unwritten stories, left untried,
Laughing at jokes where plot twists hide.

Of Dreams Left Behind

Sneakers old with squeaky soles,
Stuck in a dream of unplayed roles.
Relics of hope, gathering dust,
Waiting for laughter, a thrill, a gust.

Comfy pillows hold their dreams tight,
Whispering tales all through the night.
But mornings come with a fizzy pop,
And hopes bounce back, then take a flop.

A carousel built from mismatched thoughts,
Going in circles, aiming for spots.
Laughter and sighs weave through the air,
While hopes get tangled in yesterday's hair.

Forgotten dreams just wear a grin,
Winking at all that might have been.
In forgotten corners of our mind,
We're all just jesters, a little blind.

Threads of Yesteryear

A sweater knits tales from the past,
Stitches hold secrets, joy's forecast.
Patterns woven in giggles and snorts,
With flat-out jokes that never fall short.

Buttons of whimsy, color and cheer,
Laughter hangs on every thread near.
Each row a story, a chuckle or two,
In corners where sunlight hides from view.

Mismatched yarn wraps around the truth,
A tapestry brimming with silliness, sleuth.
In every knot, a wink does abide,
As dreams of yesterday take up a ride.

And so we wear our whims with pride,
While threads of life continue to glide.
In this fabric, history's charm,
Wraps us close in its lovable swarm.

Treasures of Unspoken Narratives

In a box, there lies a shoe,
One just one, and not a clue,
Where's the mate? It's plain to see,
A dance partner lost to memory.

An old hat with feathers bright,
Might have seen a wild night flight,
A party where the fun took wing,
Now just dust and echoes sing.

Old letters stained with coffee smears,
Confessions whispered through the years,
A love that fizzled like old soda,
Left to linger, just like Yoda.

A rubber chicken from a game,
That once brought laughter, now feels lame,
Yet in this clutter, joy remains,
In whispered tales of silly gains.

Curiosities of Past Lament

In a corner, sits a clown,
Painted smile is wearing down,
What mischief brewed when he was bold,
Now collects dust, his tale untold.

A broken toy that used to race,
Now just limps with tired grace,
Its wheels once spun like carefree days,
Now just echoes in the haze.

A teacup chipped yet filled with spice,
Holds secrets that are not so nice,
It giggles softly, leaks a tale,
Of a tea party gone quite stale.

An old calendar with days gone by,
Marks moments bold, like kittens shy,
In these remnants, laughter springs,
And every memory dances, sings.

Collecting the Fragments of Yesterday

A sock that's lost its match for years,
Tells of adventures, laughs, and tears,
Through laundry mazes, fun was fought,
Where did it wander, why it sought?

A camera lens, cracked but proud,
Captured moments that drew a crowd,
Now it sits, a bit askew,
Wondering where its friends all flew.

An empty jar, once filled with dreams,
Memories swirl like ice cream streams,
What treasures once it held with glee,
Now floats away undiscovered, free.

An old guitar, still with a tune,
Plays a lullaby to the moon,
Strummed by hands now far away,
Yet echoes of joy still stay.

Fleeting Glimmers in the Gloom

Beneath the dust, a light shines bright,
A rubber band that lost its fight,
Once a weapon in great play,
Now just ties up dreams, they say.

A tattered book of silly rhymes,
Forgotten fables of better times,
Its pages turn with laughter's breath,
In shadows, it dances, cheating death.

A jigsaw piece, one oddly shaped,
From a puzzle that the dog escaped,
Searching high and low for fun,
Hiding there, it just won't run.

A forgotten hat with a propeller,
Brought to life by a youthful feller,
Now crammed tight in a box of gloom,
It spins tales of laughter, space, and zoom.

Recollections in Dim Light

Old toys dance in the gloom,
Dust bunnies gossip in the room.
A bear wearing pants, quite a sight,
Laughs at shoes lost in the night.

A clock that ticks but never chimes,
Recites forgotten nursery rhymes.
A soapbox car waits for a race,
While rubber ducks plot their escape.

Grandpa's wig, a feathery hat,
Wanted to fly, but all it did was chat.
Bottles of laughter, jars of cheer,
Each corner holds a tale, it's clear!

As shadows play tag with the light,
The past gives a wink, what a sight!
In this kingdom of whimsy and fun,
A treasure chest of dreams, just begun.

Unraveled Dreams in the Dark

A skateboard rests on spider's thread,
Whispers of glory, but none are led.
A banner hangs, 'Best in the Show',
But the trophy's just a half-eaten scone.

A squeezy toy plays the trumpet loud,
While forgotten snacks form a proud cloud.
A sticky note with dreams so grand,
Now a paper plane, lost in hand.

The light bulb flickers with a grin,
As laughter echoes - that's how it spins!
Sock puppets chuckle, secrets keep,
In this realm where silence is sheep.

A crumpled map leads to nowhere new,
Yet hopes ride bicycles, have fun too.
In this tangled web of joy and jest,
The essence of dreams gets a comic rest.

Imaginations Sheltered from Time

A pirate ship made of old shoe boxes,
Sails on waves of mismatched socks.
The captain is a lonely cat,
With a patchwork hat that looks quite fat.

Faraway lands made from old tinfoil,
Where spoons and forks are kings, we toil.
A glue stick dragon guards the way,
A hero awaits, for fun and play.

Postcards sent from nowhere pure,
With goofy maps that twist and lure.
The best adventures come from fluff,
While binoculars made of leaves look tough.

Each cranny holds giggles and sighs,
A phantom plays peek-a-boo with the skies.
In the corners, dreams quietly squirm,
Wrapped in laughter, awaiting their turn.

Whispers in the Attic Space

In the corner, a box full of fluff,
Missed out on play, but it's still tough.
A giggle snorts from an old shoe,
Where once there lived a jolly kangaroo.

The curtain waves with a little jig,
Spinning tales of a dancing twig.
An umbrella dreams of rainy rides,
While the old typewriter still hides.

A chair that creaks tells tales of old,
Of parties once filled with laughter bold.
Marbles roll, plotting their fate,
Under a table where dreams wait.

The air is thick with humor so light,
Echoing joy into the night.
Amongst the clutter and phantom tease,
Whispers of whimsy float with ease.

Chronicles of a Silent Space

In a corner, a sock lies alone,
Its mate took flight, as dreams have flown.
Dust bunnies giggle, a playful crew,
Chasing shadows, like toddlers do.

An unkempt hat atop a forgotten chair,
Hides secrets of laughter in the stale air.
It once danced in the breeze, oh what a sight,
Now it whispers nonsense half-heartedly, right?

Old toys conspire at the break of dawn,
Waging battles where nobody's drawn.
Plastic knights and dolls join the spree,
Debating whose stories are far wittier.

A calendar laughs with a date gone wrong,
Says it's Tuesday, but it can't last long.
Each page a joke, written in haste,
Celebrating tomorrows that never took place.

Haunting Melodies of Tomorrow

An old radio hums a tune from the past,
Sings of a future that zoomed by so fast.
Its knobs are rusty, its buttons all stuck,
   Playing the hits of a luckless pluck.

Balloons float high, but one lost the fight,
   It's stuck on a nail, living life in plight.
Whispers of laughter echo through space,
As it dreams of parties that never took place.

A guitar strums softly with fingers of dust,
Its melodies haunting, but it's lost all trust.
Once it serenaded the moonlight's embrace,
   Now it complains of a lack of good taste.

Chairs clatter softly like ghosts on a spree,
   Claiming their territory with great esprit.
They argue in silence, who used to lounge,
   In this silly spectacle they form a frown.

Tattered Pages of What-Ifs

On shelves, old books gather tales that are wild,
Each storyline waiting like an unspoiled child.
Their covers are dusty, their words out of sight,
With plots that twist in the dim of the night.

One page cries out, 'What if I was read?'
'I'd take you on journeys instead of this bed!'
But all the bookmarks have long since been lost,
Each adventure stalled, counting the cost.

Ink spills like laughter on forgotten lore,
While a bookmark dreams of what's behind door four.
Characters dance in their moth-eaten gowns,
While spines bend in agony, boasting their crowns.

They murmur of life, oh so grand and bizarre,
While knitting their dreams under dust-draped stars.
Each whispering chapter sighs with a grin,
Knowing the adventures could start with a spin.

Ghosts of Ambition's Remains

A dusty typewriter clacks in despair,
Longing for stories that vanish in air.
It rustles old papers with ink stains of woe,
Pleading for patience where ideas can grow.

Dreams of grandeur float high like a kite,
But stuck in a cyclone of sleep-walking night.
Each paperclip thinks it's a grand sorceress,
Bending the rules of this slow wilderness.

Old coats hang low, tales draped on the rack,
Murmuring softly, 'We won't take the flak!'
Each pocket holds wishes, some bright, some absurd,
But all are forgotten, not once even stirred.

A clock ticks away; seconds drift like sand,
Counting ambitions that never quite planned.
Yet voices of hope slip through like a dream,
Laughing together in this whimsical scheme.

Shadows of Silenced Ambitions

In a corner, dust bunnies lie,
Whispering hopes that are shy.
They giggle and snicker, quite bold,
Of journeys not taken, stories untold.

A tricycle waits for a ride,
While dreams on a shelf take a side.
The teddy bear shakes off the dust,
And ponders why nobody trusts.

A rocket ship made of old cheese,
Plans to venture, if you please!
But the cat just naps in the way,
While the dreams fight for light of day.

Old magazines stacked up so high,
Look back and wonder, oh my!
They chuckle at paths never roamed,
In a place where ambition is honed.

Vault of Lost Aspirations

An umbrella hangs with a frown,
Tired of never being put down.
It dreams of rainstorms from the past,
But merely collects dust, unsurpassed.

Sneakers worn from countless plans,
Wishing for walks on sunny sands.
Yet here they sit in a pile so high,
Waiting for someone to give it a try.

A cookbook filled with recipes wild,
Hiding in shadows, feeling defiled.
Pancakes once dreamed with fluffy flair,
Now half-forgotten, beyond repair.

A globe spins with a wheel of fate,
Yearning for places, it can't quite sate.
It whispers, "Let's roll, don't just stare,"
But all that it gets is a dusty glare.

Secrets Beneath the Eaves

A spider spins webs of regret,
Hanging secrets you can't forget.
Old shoes with tales to share,
About adventures, but no one's there.

Boxes bursting with laughter and tears,
Haunted by days, years, and years.
They giggle as they stir the air,
While reality gives a vacant stare.

An old radio crackles a tune,
Of dreams that once danced to the moon.
It sighs for the music that's gone,
In the echoing silence, forlorn.

Curtains draw in a playful play,
On shadows of wishes that sway.
They poke fun at aspirations gone,
In a cupboard where hopes linger on.

Ghosts of Unborn Possibilities

In the back, where wild ideas dwell,
Shush, they huddle and tell.
Of what ifs and maybes that fell,
To chase after sparks, in dreams they rebel.

A bicycle rusts beneath the beams,
Yearning for roads and sunlight beams.
It chuckles, "Just give me a chance,"
While dust settles and leaves no dance.

A board game with pieces mislaid,
Where hopes and laughs once played.
Now just sits, waiting for fun,
On a path where ambitions run.

In this realm of faded plans,
The ghosts pop out with their silly cans.
Shaking their heads at what could be,
In a nook where dreams run wild and free.

Chronicles of Unlived Tomorrows

In a box where socks go to play,
Lies a world of plans gone astray.
Fuzzy ideas, all tangled and spun,
Hiding from daylight, just having fun.

There's a dream of flying on a broom,
Imaginary cats are plotting in gloom.
A recipe lost, for never-made pie,
Just dust and crumbs, oh me, oh my!

The calendar's pages, stuck in one place,
Laugh at the goals that left not a trace.
An old disco ball spins on the shelf,
Reflecting the dreams we forgot ourselves.

So let's toast to plans that never took flight,
And the quirky dreams that still make us light.
For in every chuckle at past mistakes,
Lies a joy that every memory makes.

Secrets Buried Under Time's Rug.

Under the rug where old dust bunnies thrive,
Secrets are plotting to come back alive.
A dancing pickle, a hat made of cheese,
Wonders of nonsense that aim to please.

A pair of shoes with stories to spill,
Arguing with slippers that give them a thrill.
The ghost of a sandwich, all gooey and bold,
Whispers of flavors, long-told but not sold.

A pillow fort kingdom of fuzzy delight,
Where missing socks rule the world every night.
A box of regrets, but in fun shapes and hues,
Coz sometimes we win when we just cannot lose.

So shake out that rug, let the secrets all flow,
Embrace the absurd, let the laughter just grow.
For in this wild ballroom of whimsy and fun,
The dance of the forgotten has just begun.

Whispers of Abandoned Wishes

In a jar of old marbles, dreams slip and slide,
Whispers of wishes that once took a ride.
A unicycle yearning for wheels that don't roll,
Alongside a sock puppet with too much soul.

A kite stuck in branches, it longs for the sky,
While doodles of monsters just giggle nearby.
A jigsaw of laughter, missing a piece,
A puzzle of joys that never find peace.

Dreams of a rocket made from a spoon,
Set sail for the stars beneath a big moon.
Yet here they all linger, just fine-tuning plans,
To launch all their fun with imaginary fans.

So listen for echoes of wishes gone shy,
In the chorus of laughter, oh me, oh my!
For every small giggle, and each cheerful cheer,
Holds the secret to wishes that still linger near.

Echoes of Dusty Fantasies

In a chest full of trinkets from long, long ago,
Echoes of whims still giggle and glow.
A pirate ship sailing through laundry piled high,
With a crew made of socks that just want to fly.

A rubber chicken dreams of stardom, you see,
Adorning the stage of a grand comedy.
While a forgotten skateboard collects its old dust,
Wishing for glory—or perhaps just some thrust.

A fortune cookie that never got cracked,
Holds secrets of laughter, all perfectly packed.
A smoothie of ideas in a blender that spits,
Mixing desire with whimsical hits.

So gather your chuckles, let memories spark,
For each laugh we share leaves a beautiful mark.
In the realm of the silly, where dreams never die,
We find joy in the dust as we giggle and fly.

Breath of Forgotten Promises

In a corner, dust bunnies play,
Whispering hopes that just went away.
Once they danced with glee and charm,
Now they hide, causing no alarm.

A photo of a taco hat,
Claiming fame, how about that?
It promised style, a fashion spree,
But just collects dust, oh silly me.

Old shoes sit dreaming of the road,
Worn and weary, carrying their load.
They promised runs, the wind and fun,
Yet now they loaf, the race is done.

A broken kite without a string,
Once it soared, oh the joy it brings!
Now grounded, it yearns for the sky,
A forgotten dream, oh me, oh my!

Nebulas of Distant Aspirations

A telescope stares at stars afar,
Hoping dreams will land like a shooting star.
But instead, it spies a frying pan,
Wondering how it all began.

Books stacked high, like Jenga they sway,
Whispering 'read me' in a funny way.
They once had tales of grandest quests,
Now they plot naps, like wise little pests.

An old bike rusting with a frown,
Once raced the wind, now just sits down.
It promised to take me on great rides,
Now it laughs as my ambition hides.

A rocket made of glitter and glue,
Set for the moon, but stuck with a screw.
It dreams of blasting with vibrant zeal,
But instead it's a toy for the surreal.

Secret Rooms of Old Desires

Behind the door, a closet of dreams,
Holds crayons and glitter, or so it seems.
It promised art, but rolls of tape,
Now create sculptures, a cardboard shape.

A stuffed bear with a very saggy hug,
Once a hero, now just a shrug.
He promised bravery, sunsets in gold,
But now he's a pillow, silent and old.

Forgotten wishes in a dusty vase,
Whispering secrets that time can't erase.
They giggle at plans that went awry,
Waiting for hope to give them a try.

A jar of marbles, lost in the fray,
Once rolled high, now stuck in clay.
They dreamed of races with a sweet woo-hoo,
But settled for stories, just me and you.

The Light That Once Shined Bright

A lamp with a flicker, oh what a tease,
Promised warmth, now it just wheezes.
It longed to brighten my cozy nights,
Now it plays games, like power fights.

A dance floor of mismatched old shoes,
Where dreams two-stepped, now they snooze.
Once they sparkled, now they just lie,
Waiting for a shoe fairy, oh me, oh my!

A board game with rules learned in June,
But now sits quiet, like an old tune.
It promised laughter, thrills, and fun,
But now the pieces have all but run.

Postcards from places unknown all blend,
Reminders of journeys that never had end.
They echo tales of adventures grand,
Now serving as coasters, oh how they stand!

www.ingramcontent.com/pod-product-compliance
Lightning Source LLC
Chambersburg PA
CBHW060146230426
43661CB00003B/596